The Open-String Book

for Viola

by Cassia Harvey

CHP250

©2014 by C. Harvey Publications All Rights Reserved.

www.charveypublications.com - print books
www.learnstrings.com - PDF downloadable books
www.harveystringarrangements.com - chamber music

The Open-String Book for Viola

1. Open A String

2. Open A with Rests

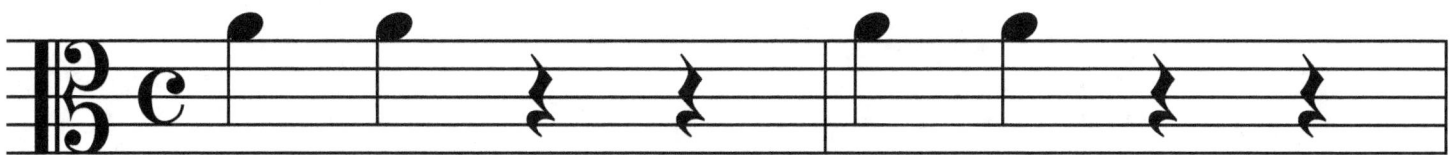

©2014 C. Harvey Publications All Rights Reserved.

3. Open A with More Rests

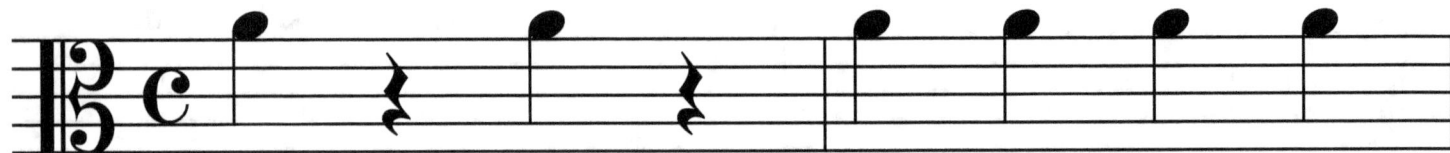
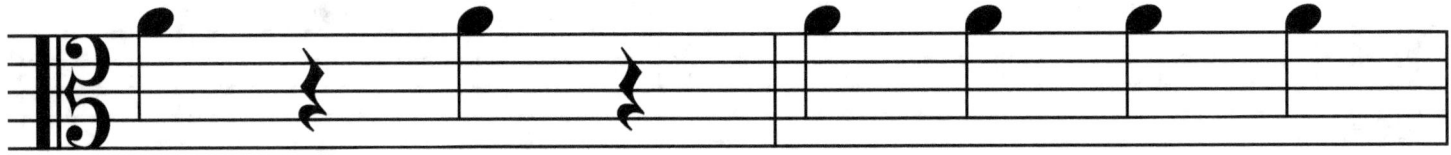
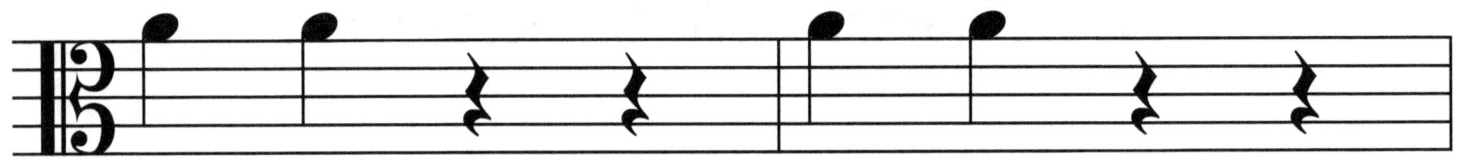

4. Open D String

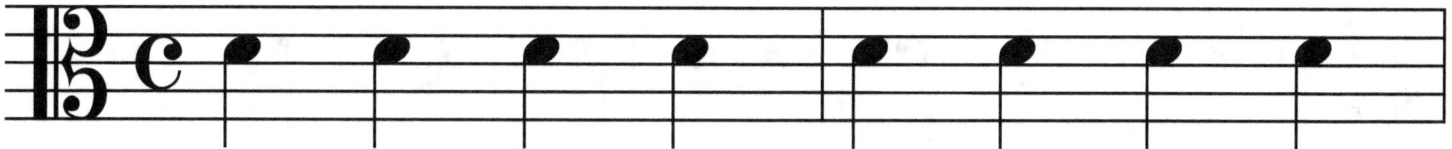

5. Open D with Long-Short-Short

6. Open D with Rests

7. Open D with Half Notes

8. Open A and D

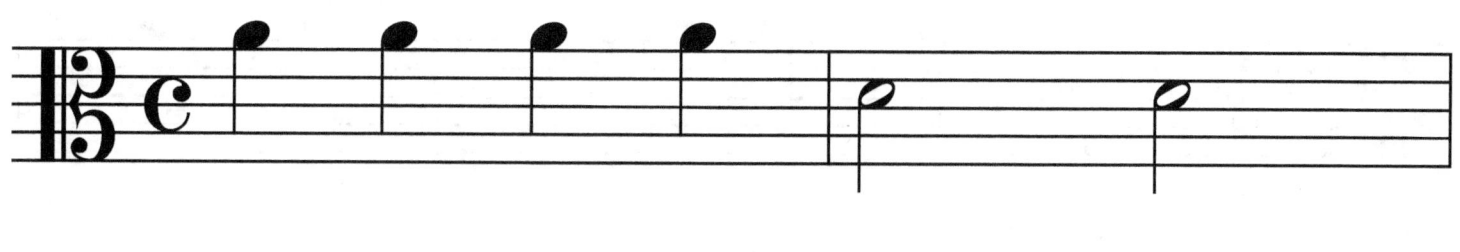

9. Open A and D Double Stops

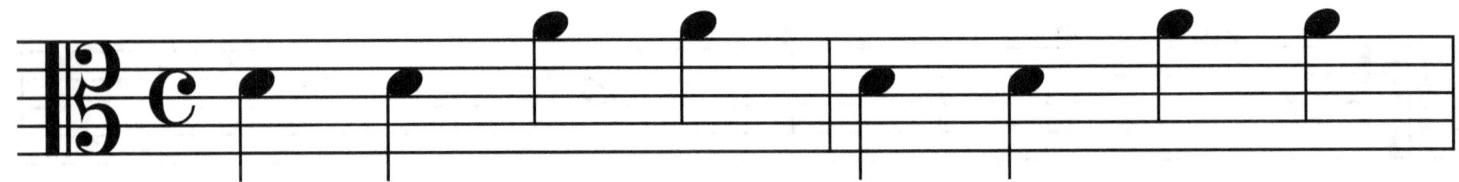

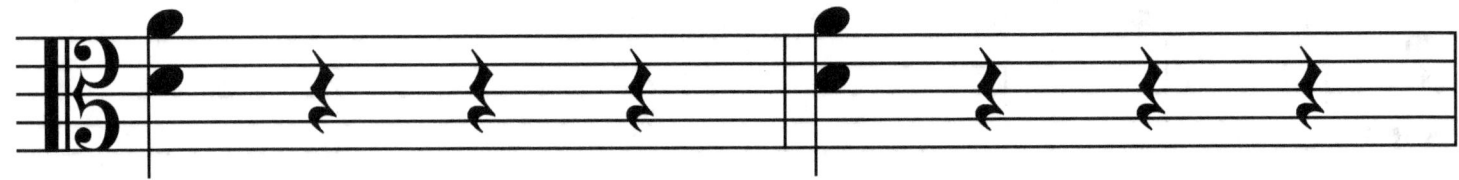

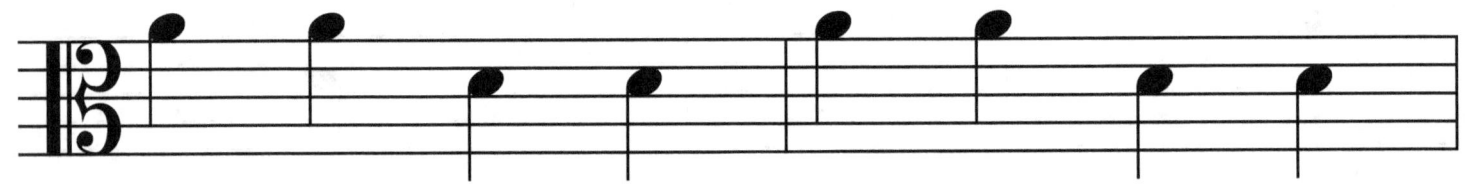

10. Open G String

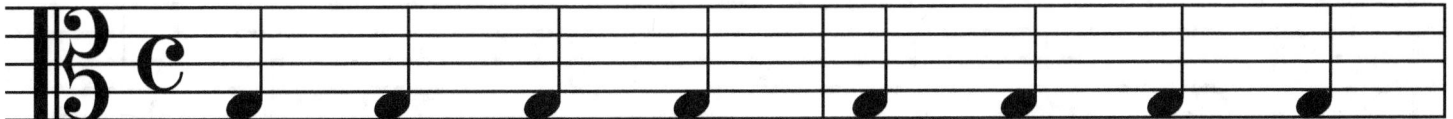

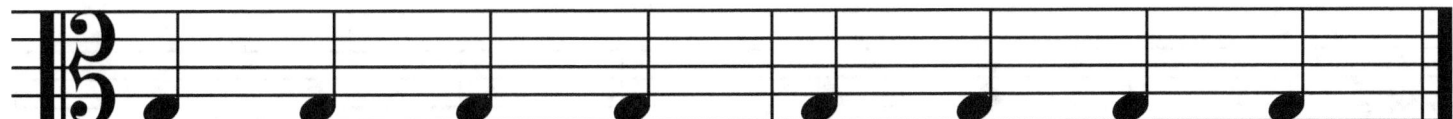

11. Open G with Short-Short-Long

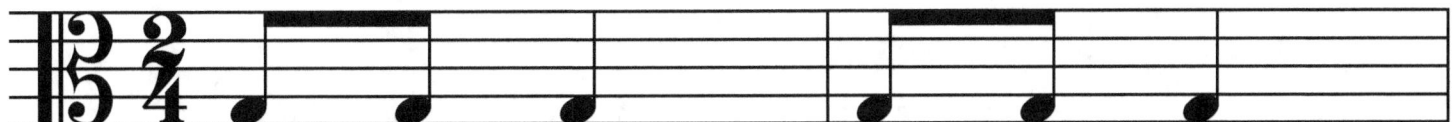

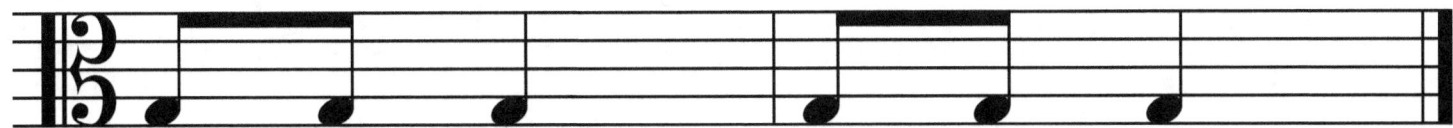

12. Open G with Rests

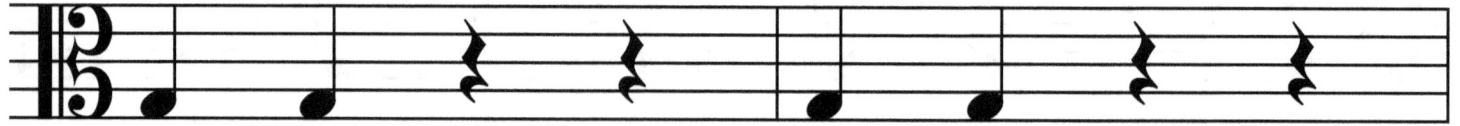
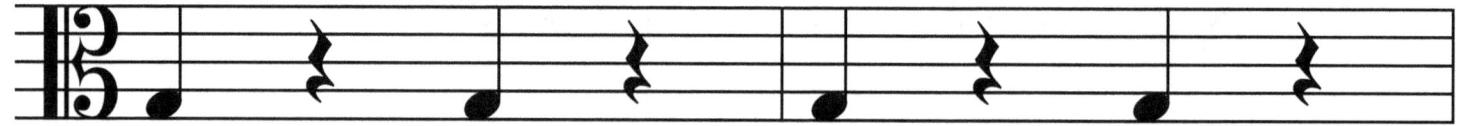
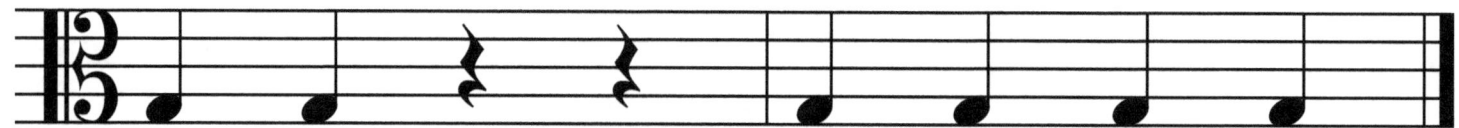

13. Open G and D

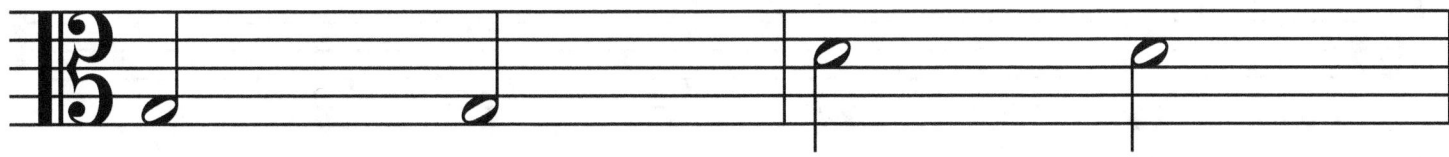
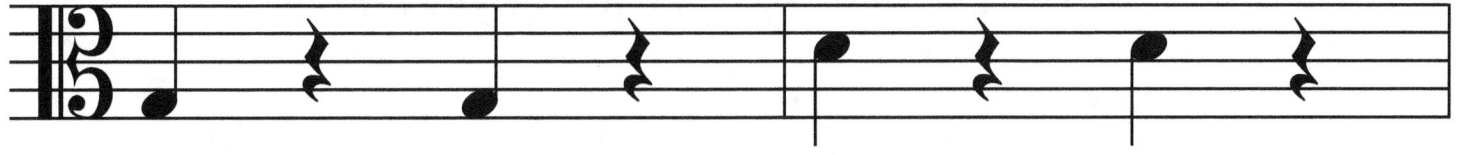
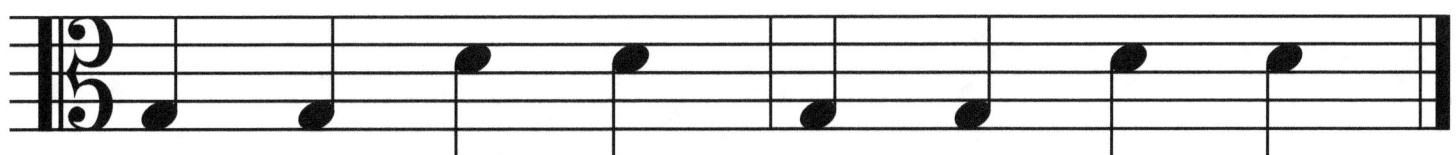

14. Open C

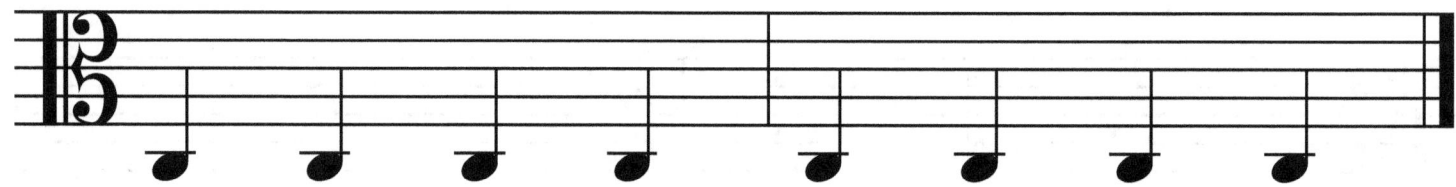

15. Open C with Rests

16. Open C with Short-Short-Long

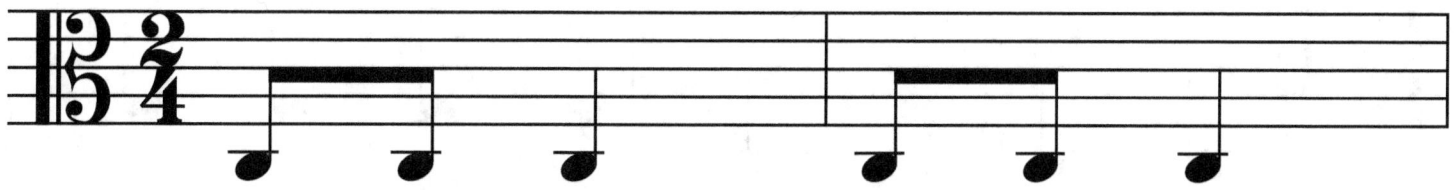

17. Open C and G

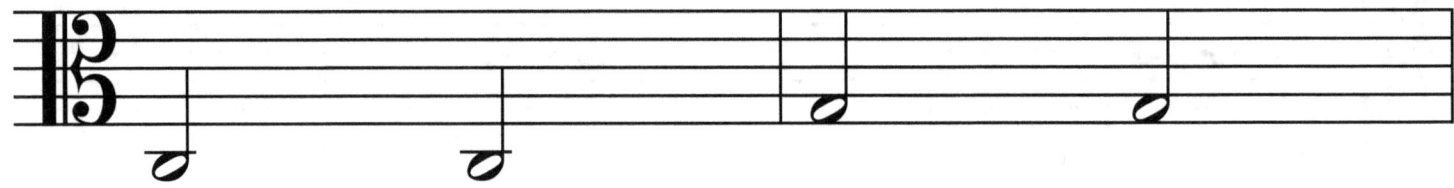

18. Double Stops on A and D

19. Double Stops on D and G

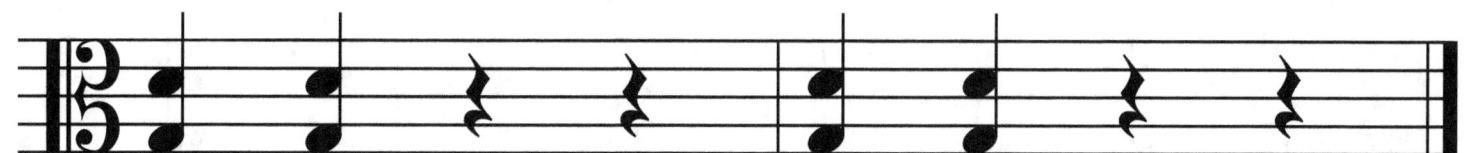

20. Double Stops on G and C

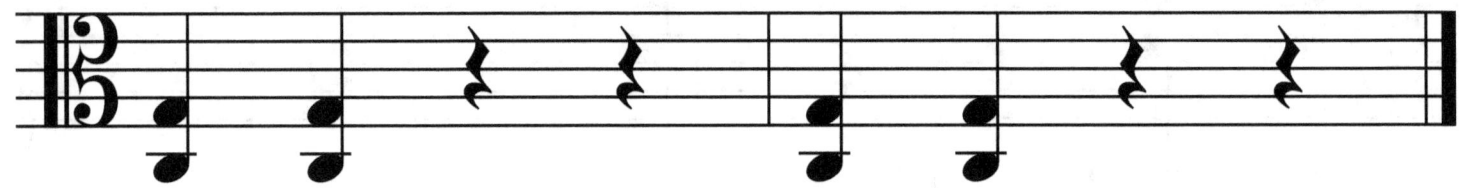

21. Marching in Double Stops

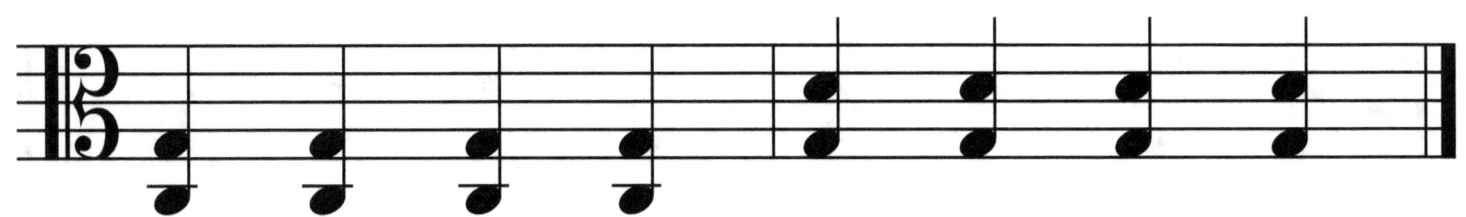

22. Counting to 3

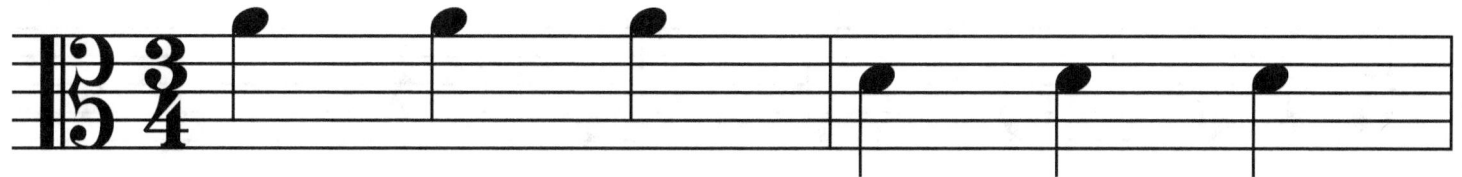
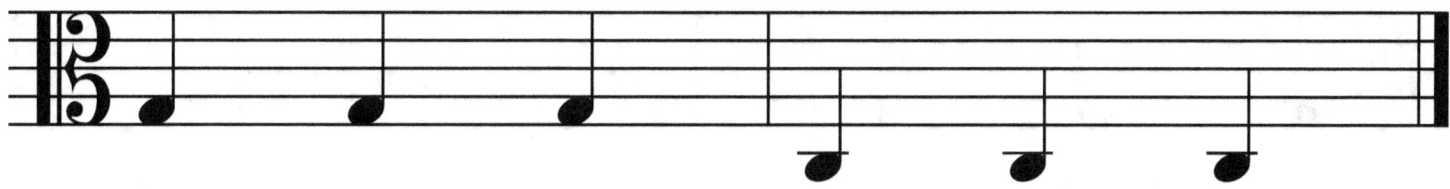

23. Three Beats in a Measure

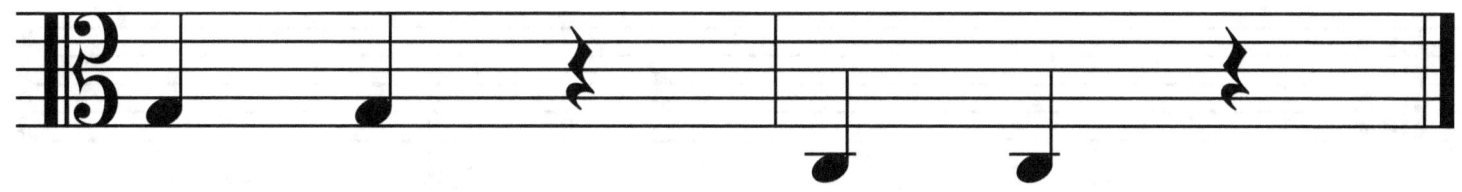

24. Three Beats on G

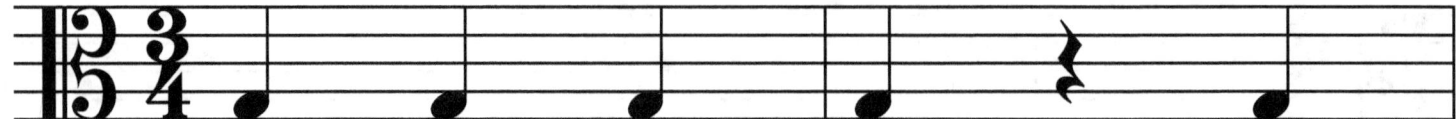

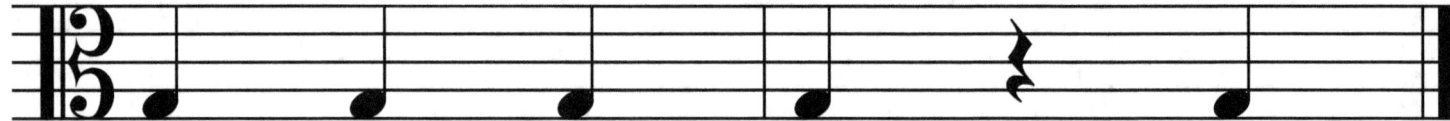

25. Three Beats on C

26. Three Beats in a Measure

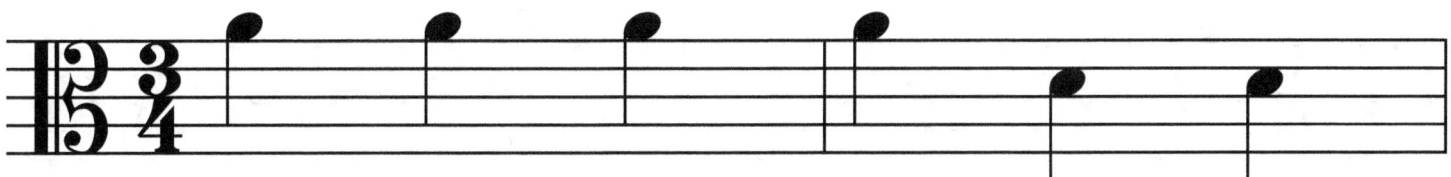
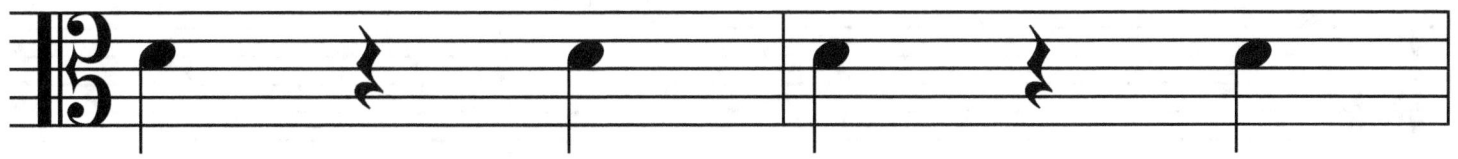

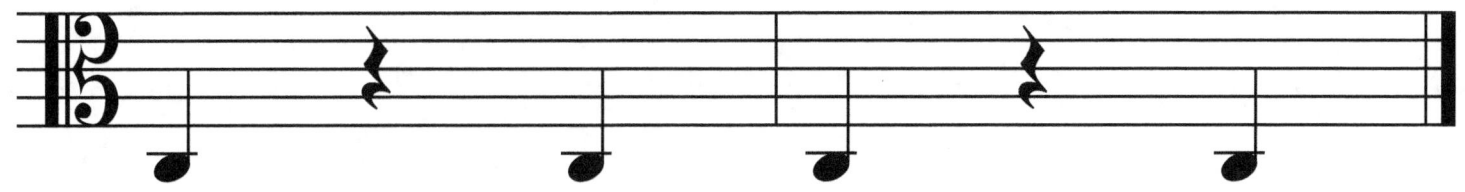

27. Two in a Bow on A and D

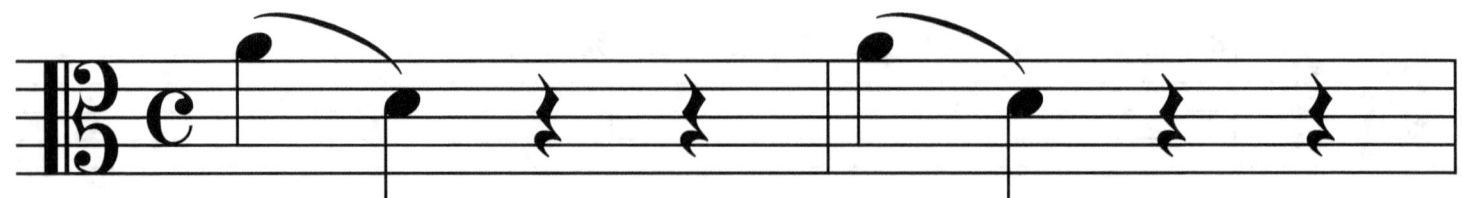

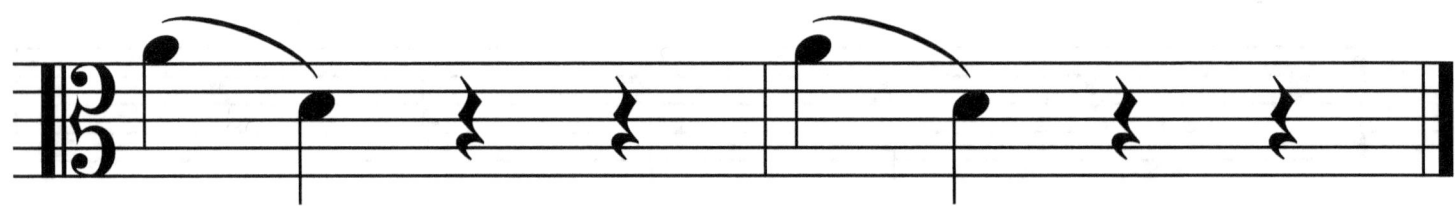

28. Two in a Bow on D and G

29. Two in a Bow on G and C

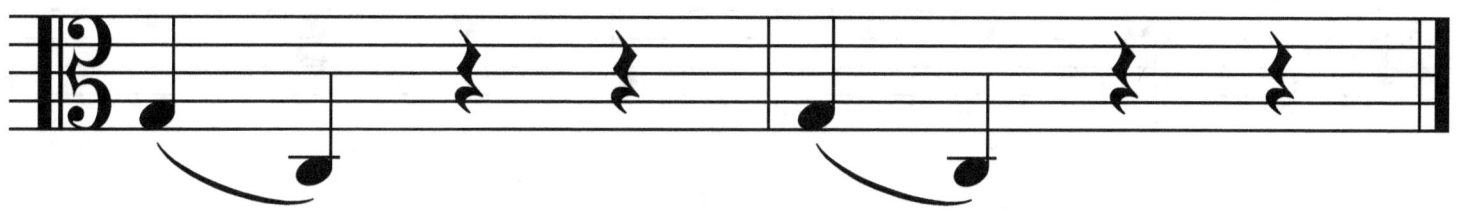

30. Two in a Bow on D and A

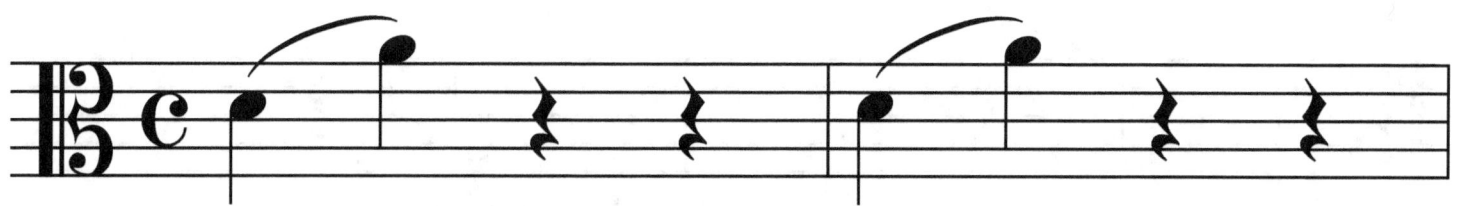

31. Two in a Bow on G and D

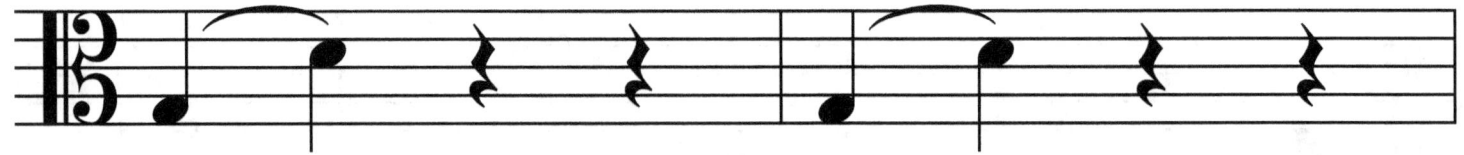

32. Two in a Bow on C and G

33. Two in a Bow without Rests

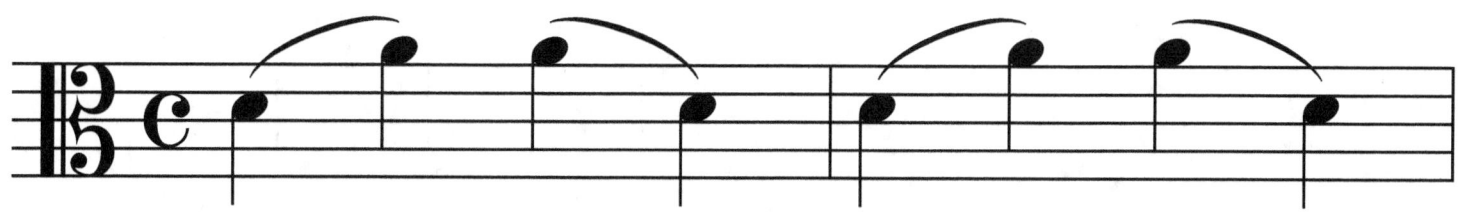

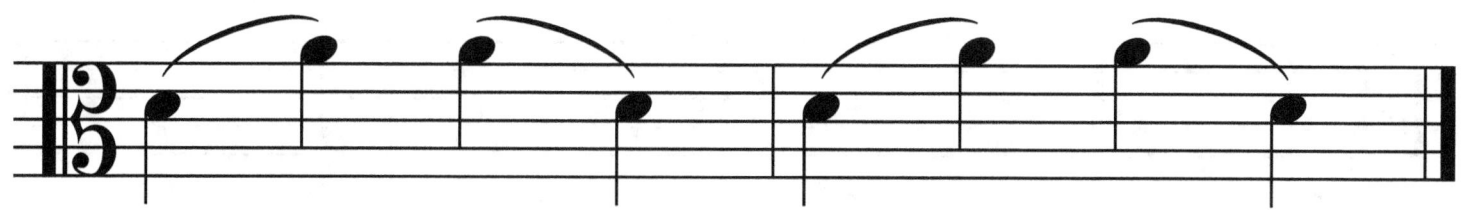

34. Two in a Bow on G and D

35. Two in a Bow on C and G

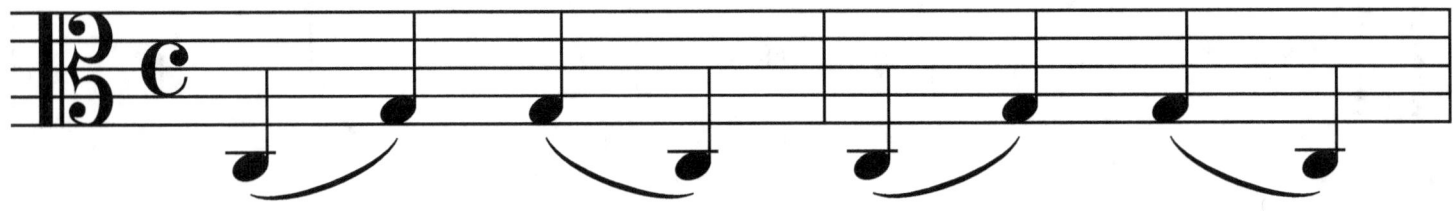

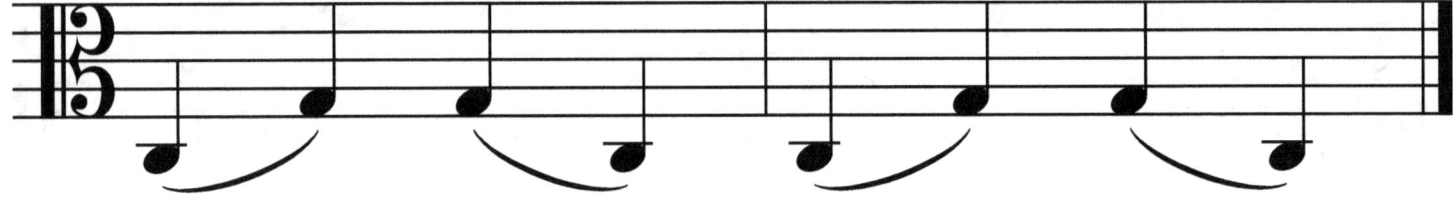

36. Slow and Fast Bows on G and C

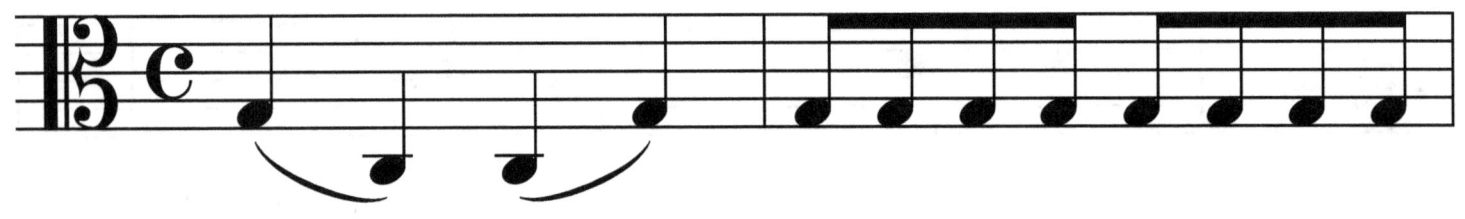

37. Slow and Fast Bows on D and G

38. Slow and Fast Bows on A and D

39. Two in a Bow Exercise

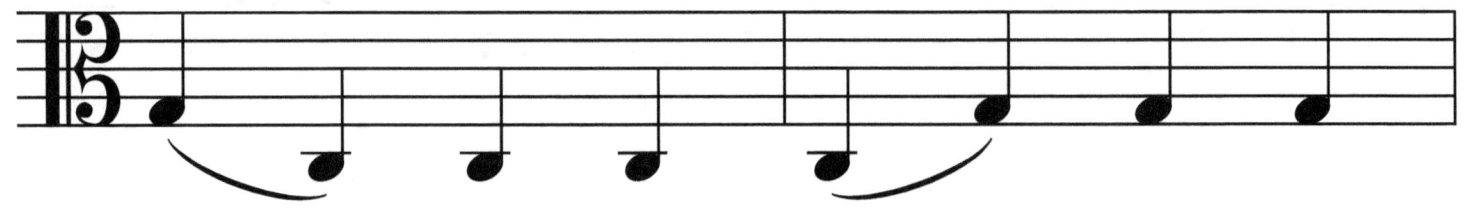
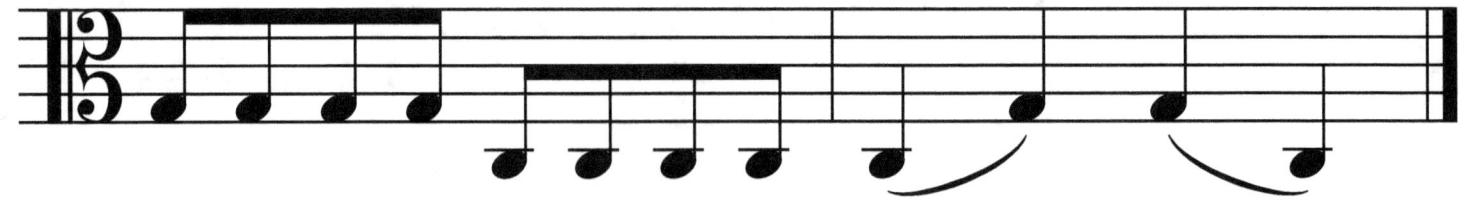

40. Whole Notes

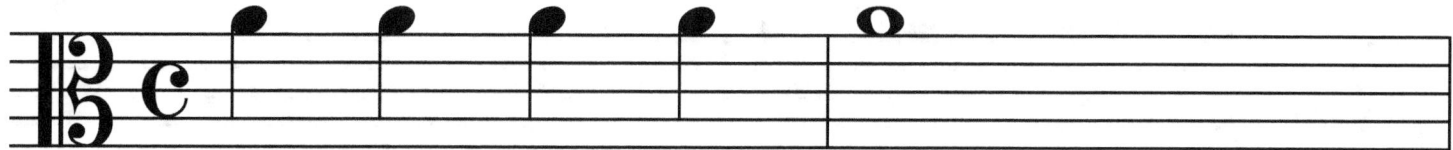

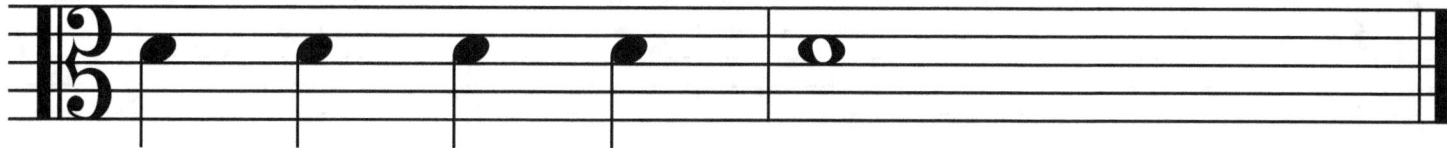

41. Half Notes and Whole Notes

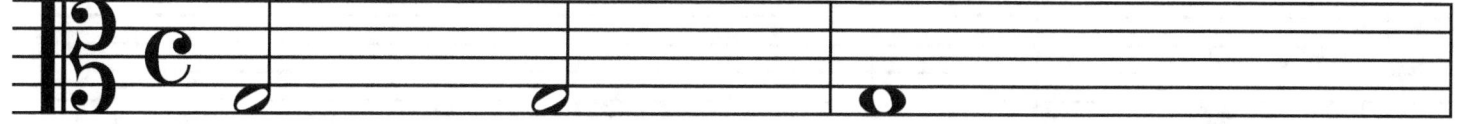

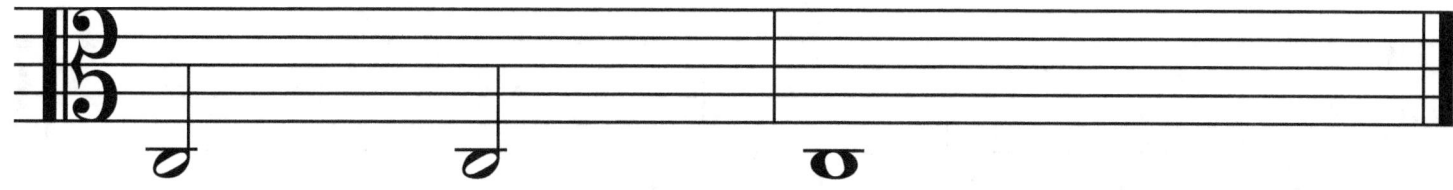

42. Counting to 1, 2, and 4

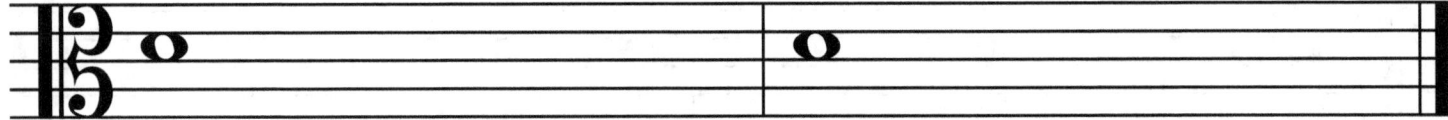

43. Counting to 1, 2, and 4

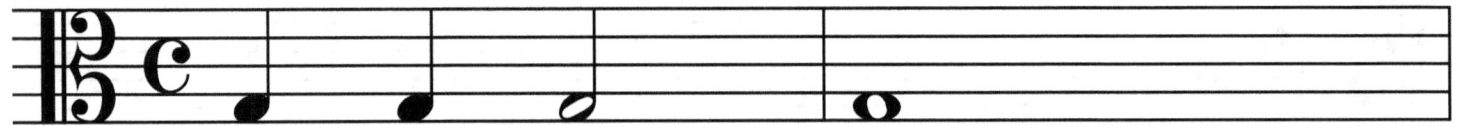

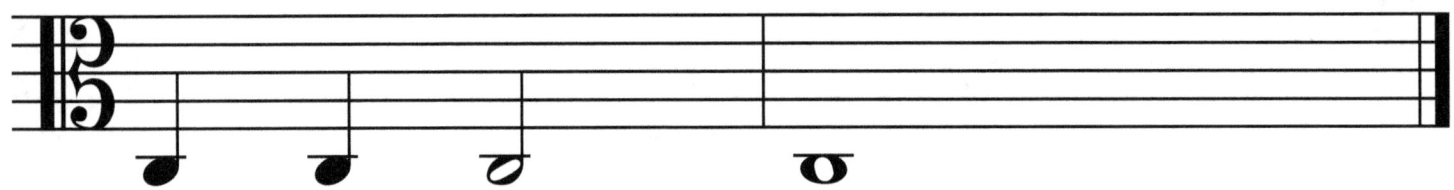

44. Counting to 1, 2, and 4

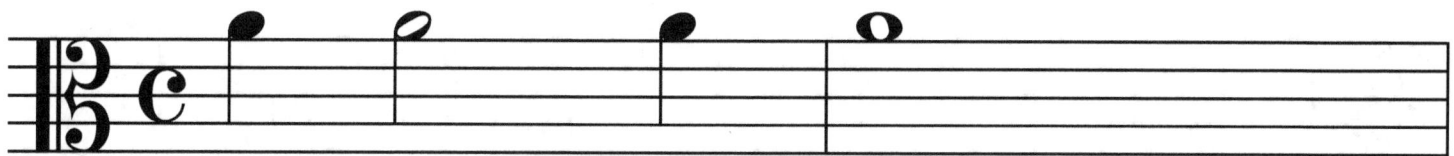

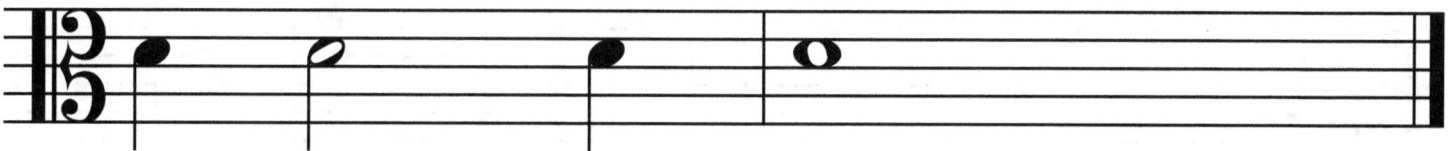

45. Counting to 1, 2, and 4

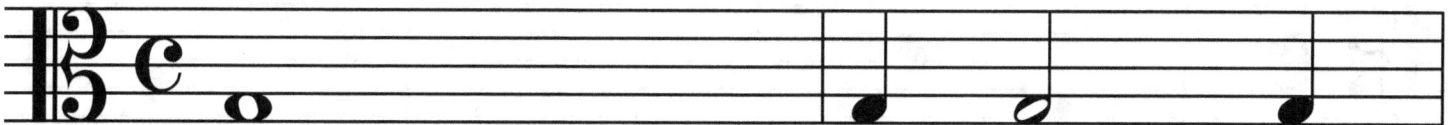

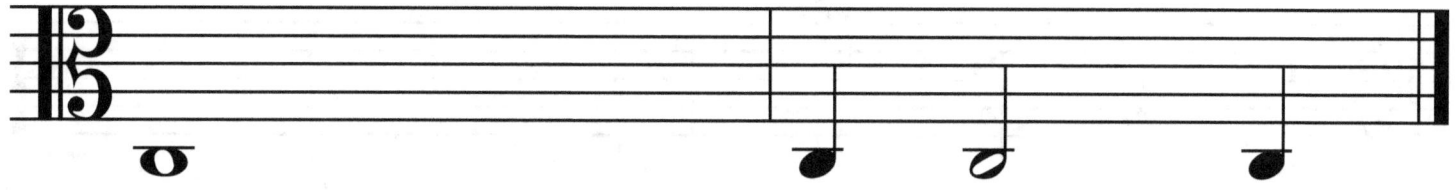

46. Counting and String Crossing

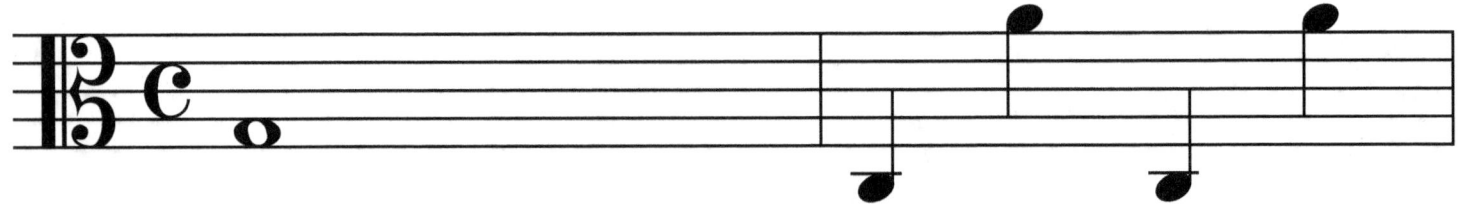

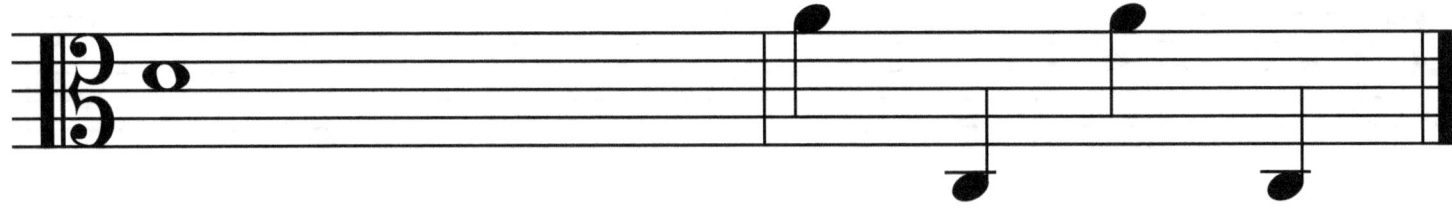

47. More Counting and String Crossing

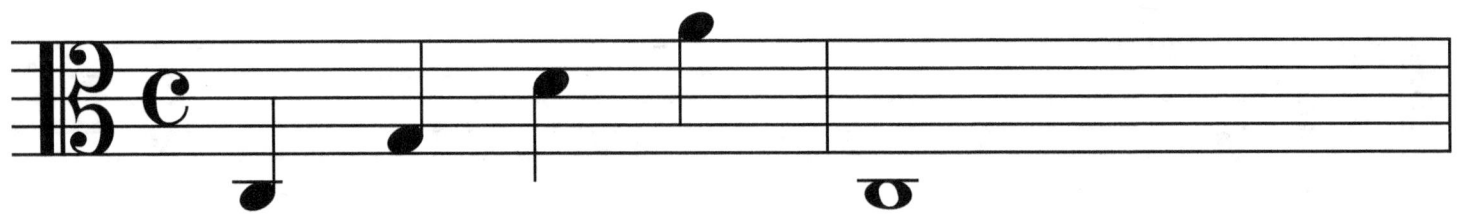

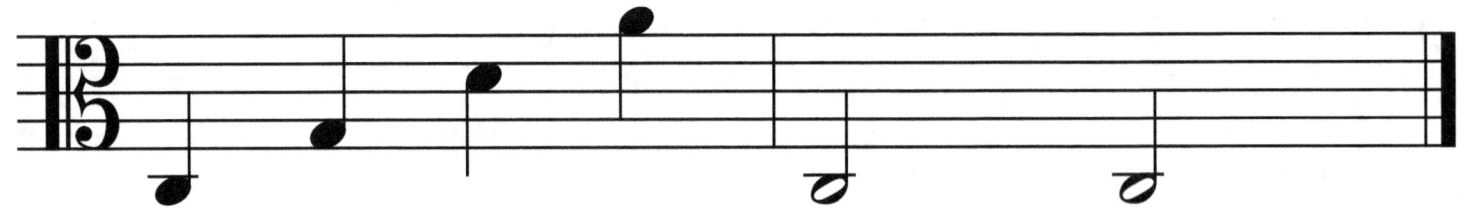

48. Putting it all Together on A and D

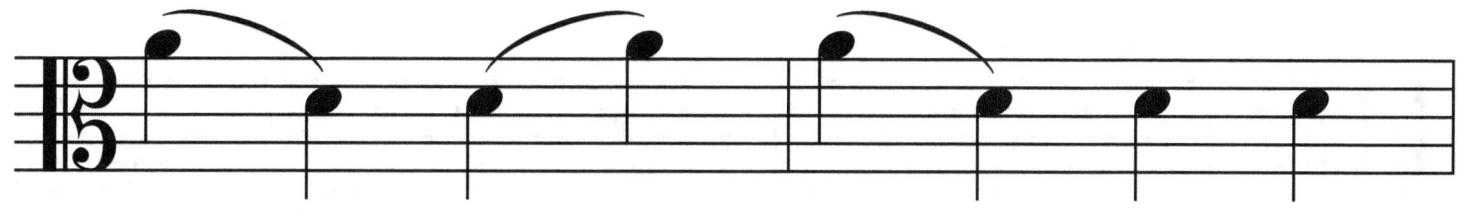

49. Putting it all Together on D and G

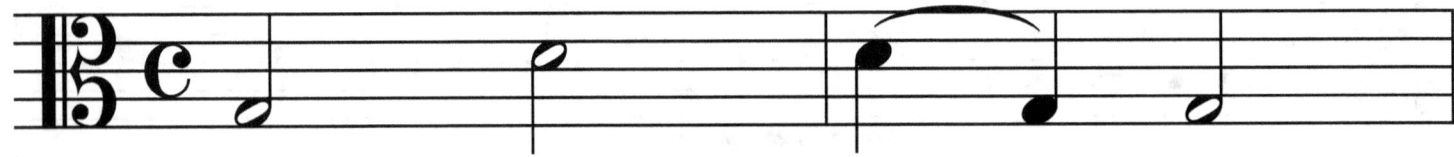

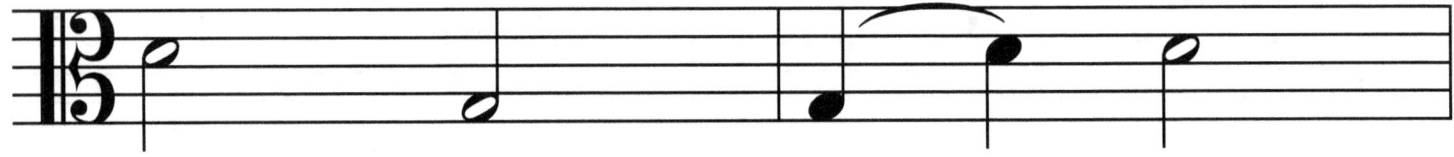

50. Putting it all Together on G and C

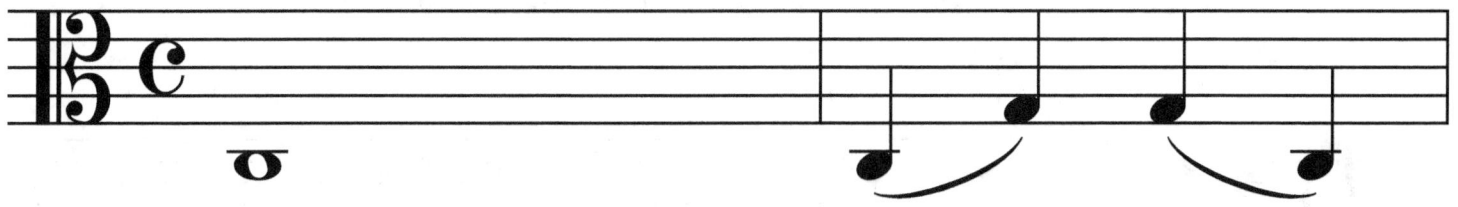

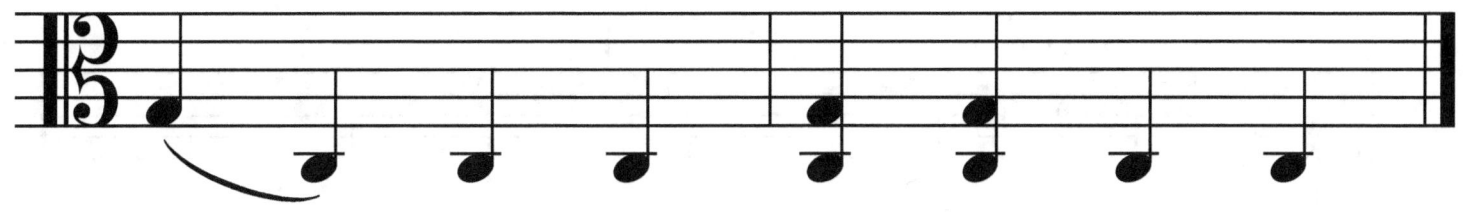

The 'Mary Had a Little Lamb' Book for Viola

1. Mary Had a Little Lamb

2. Mary Had Some Whole Notes

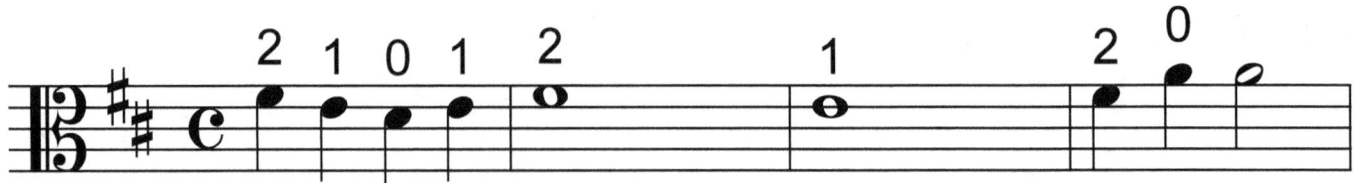

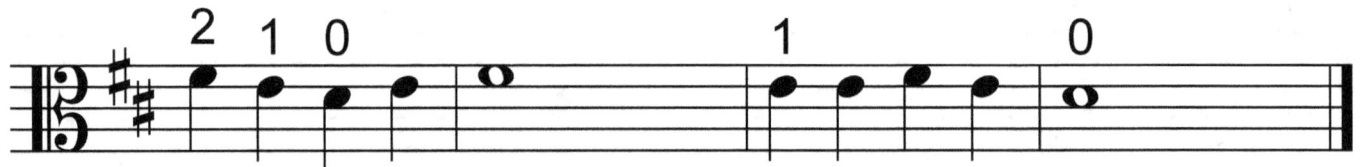

©2006 C. Harvey Publications All Rights Reserved.

www.ingramcontent.com/pod-product-compliance
Lightning Source LLC
Chambersburg PA
CBHW051429070526
44584CB00023B/3646